Tim Berners-Lee

Inventor of the World Wide Web

Heather Moore Niver

PowerKiDS press.

New York

Published in 2017 by The Rosen Publishing Group, Inc.
29 East 21st Street, New York, NY 10010

First Edition

Editor: Caitlin McAneney
Book Design: Mickey Harmon

Photo Credits: Cover, pp. 1, 3–14, 16, 18–32 (background) yxowert/Shutterstock.com; cover, pp. 5, 25 (Tim Berners-Lee) drserg/Shutterstock.com; pp. 7, 27 Science & Society Picture Library/Contributor/ SSPL/Getty Images; p. 9 Courtesy of Edward Foley/Flickr; p. 11 The Enthusiast Network/Contributor/ Getty Images; p. 13 atiger/Shutterstock.com; p. 15 Keystone/Stringer/Hulton Archives/Getty Images; p. 17 https://upload.wikimedia.org/wikipedia/commons/9/90/CERN-aerial_1.jpg; p. 19 Catrina Genovese/Contributor/Hulton Archive/Getty Images; p. 21 Boston Globe/Contributor/Getty Images; p. 23 Courtesy of ITUTimeline/Flickr; p. 29 Courtesy of Alex Lloyd/The World Wide Web Foundation.

Library of Congress Cataloging-in-Publication Data

Niver, Heather Moore, author.
 Tim Berners-Lee : inventor of the world wide web / Heather Moore Niver.
     pages cm. — (Computer pioneers)
 Includes index.
 ISBN 978-1-5081-4836-4 (pbk.)
 ISBN 978-1-5081-4772-5 (6 pack)
 ISBN 978-1-5081-4805-0 (library binding)
 1. Berners-Lee, Tim—Juvenile literature. 2. Computer scientists—Great Britain—Biography—Juvenile litera-
ture. 3. World Wide Web—History—Juvenile literature. I. Title.
 QA76.2.B48N58 2017
 025.042092—dc23
                                        2015036123

Manufactured in the United States of America

CPSIA Compliance Information: Batch #BS16PK: For Further Information contact Rosen Publishing, New York, New York at 1-800-237-9932

Contents

The Wonderful World Wide Web

Many people think Tim Berners-Lee invented the Internet—a new frontier of computer technology. However, when Berners-Lee is asked if this is true, he's quick to set the record straight. He says his work just made use of technology that was already around. This allowed Berners-Lee to create the World Wide Web (WWW).

The web is a big part of our lives today. In fact, most young people have never lived in a world without it. You can use the web to do research for a school project, connect with friends, or check your school's calendar. None of this would be possible if not for the man who would eventually be known as the Father of the Web: Tim Berners-Lee.

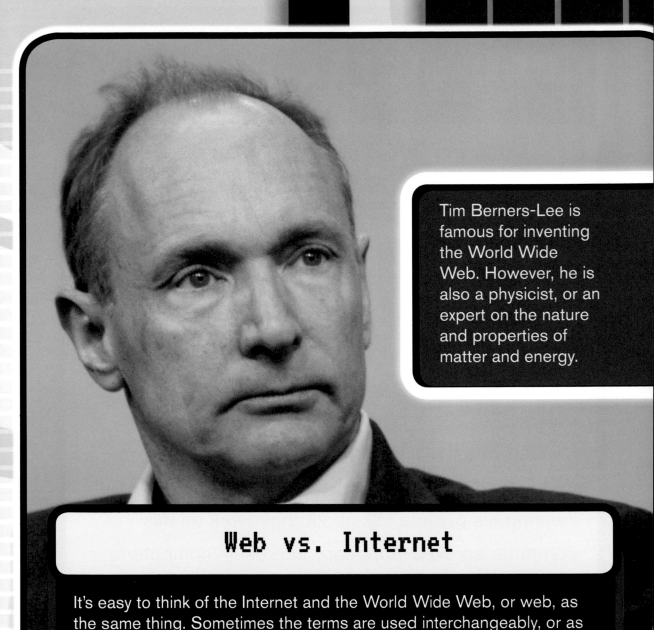

Tim Berners-Lee is famous for inventing the World Wide Web. However, he is also a physicist, or an expert on the nature and properties of matter and energy.

Web vs. Internet

It's easy to think of the Internet and the World Wide Web, or web, as the same thing. Sometimes the terms are used interchangeably, or as though one word means the same as the other. But the web and the Internet are actually very different things. The World Wide Web is a part of the Internet. The Internet is a huge network of networks that connects millions of computers to share information. The web is a way to **access** that information.

5

Computers and Books

On June 8, 1955, Timothy John Berners-Lee was born in London, England. At that time, most people had never even seen a computer! Yet he'd go on to change our world in ways we could hardly have thought possible.

Tim has three siblings—Pete, Helen, and Mike. His parents, Mary Lee Woods and Conway Berners-Lee, were mathematicians. They talked about math all the time. They both worked on the Ferranti Mark I, which was the first **commercial** computer. Tim's mother was one of the first computer programmers. Hearing his parents talk about their work on this computer sparked Tim's early interest in computers. His parents also encouraged him to read a lot and discouraged him from watching television. They taught him to have fun with math and science.

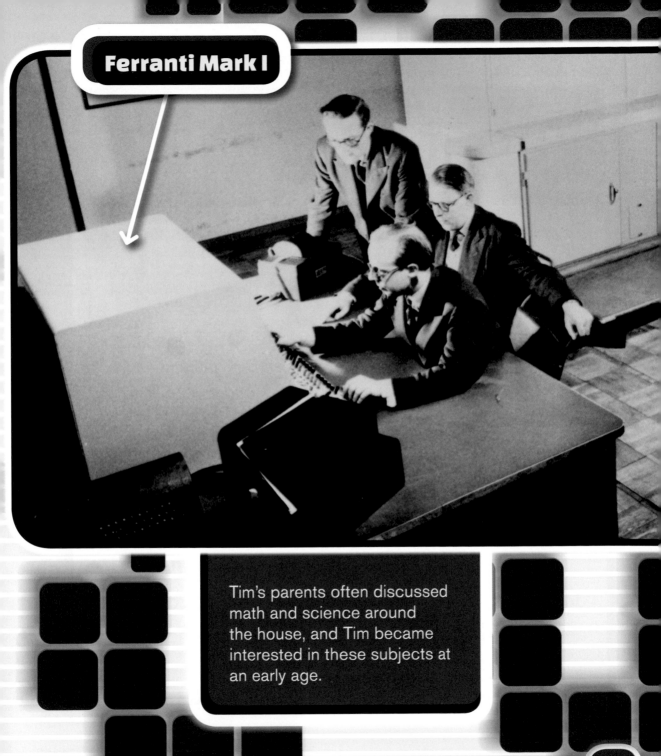

Ferranti Mark I

Tim's parents often discussed math and science around the house, and Tim became interested in these subjects at an early age.

His First Invention

When Tim was around five years old, his father took him to work. Tim got to see the computer his dad was working on. At the time, computers were not the small, personal machines we have today. He remembers it as a "a big cabinet with a clock on it, and with a desk with a paper tape reader. One box which was a paper tape reader and one box which was a paper tape punch." Tim went home and made his own "computer," using his desk, a clock, and cardboard boxes.

In elementary school, Tim and two friends decided to write a book. First, they decided to dig an underground lab for writing. It was this kind of imagination that shaped who he became.

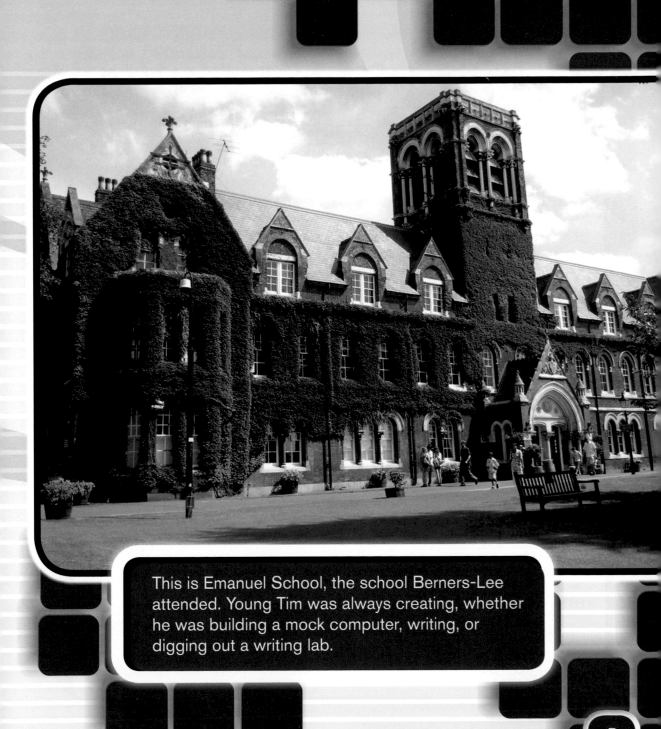

This is Emanuel School, the school Berners-Lee attended. Young Tim was always creating, whether he was building a mock computer, writing, or digging out a writing lab.

Trains and Electronics

Tim rode the train to Emanuel School, which was actually located between two sets of train tracks. With a constant reminder of trains, many boys, including Tim, became interested in model trains. Tim followed new advances in **transistors**. He and his friends would buy rejected transistors, which came in bags of 500. At home, they would test them, looking for some that worked. The boys used the working transistors to make small **circuits**. Tim built special controls for his model trains.

Tim started getting more interested in the electronics that made his trains do cool things, such as switch tracks, blow their whistles, and turn on and off. Tim would continue to follow his fascination for electronics—and computers—when he went off to college.

Tim and many of his schoolmates were always thinking about trains and how to make their model trains more exciting.

Creations at College

Berners-Lee enrolled at the University of Oxford as a **physics** student, but he also continued to inspect and experiment with electronics just for fun. He really started to get into computers when he was at Oxford. Once, during his free time, he **soldered** together a computer terminal from an old calculator, a car battery, and broken television sets!

During his Oxford days, Berners-Lee got himself in a little trouble. First, he misused the school's printer. After that, he wasn't allowed to use it. Another time, he accessed the nuclear physics laboratory's **mainframe** without proper permission. In short, he was caught hacking. He was banned from the physics lab computer, but this experience only inspired him to make a computer of his own.

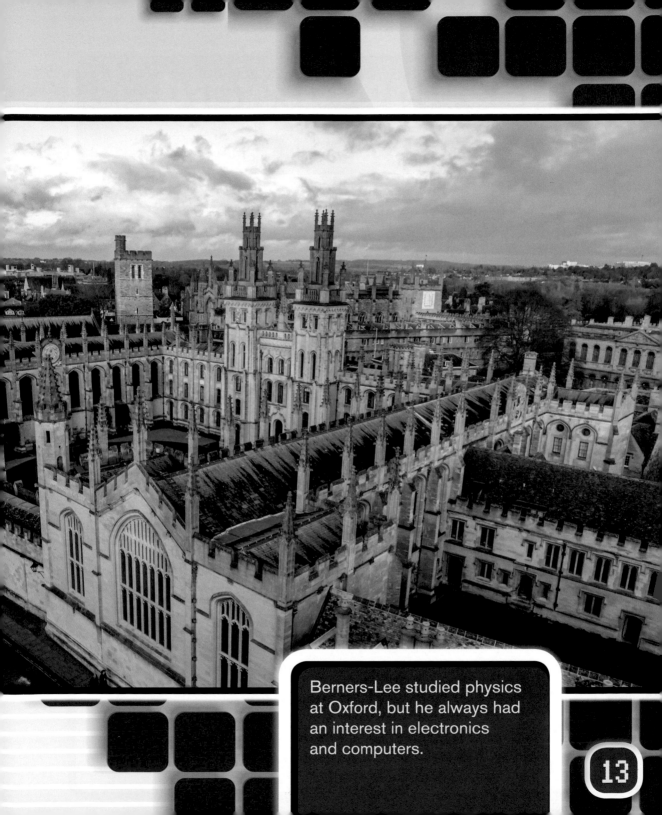

Berners-Lee studied physics at Oxford, but he always had an interest in electronics and computers.

Moving Forward with Forth

Thanks to his experimentation with computers, Berners-Lee taught himself a lot about computer languages. He even created his own simple computer languages. Then, a friend told him about a computer language called Forth. He used Forth and even improved on it, designing a language he called 10PL. By the time he graduated from college, his skills were in high demand.

Berners-Lee graduated from Oxford's Queen's College with a degree in physics in 1976 and went to work for the Plessey Company—a **telecommunications** company in Dorset, England. Berners-Lee's job was to design **software** for the company. He worked there for two years. After a few more jobs within the computer industry, he went to work at a place called CERN, which originally stood for Conseil Européen pour la Recherche Nucléaire, in 1980.

At the Plessey Company, Tim Berners-Lee gained more experience creating software. This is Plessey's computer, being used by a technician.

Making His Mark at CERN

CERN is the European **particle physics** laboratory that's located in Geneva, Switzerland. Berners-Lee's work at CERN didn't seem to start out as anything remarkable. While he was there, he had to organize research from a bunch of different teams from all over the world. The teams were all using different computer systems for their work.

Berners-Lee created a program for himself that he called Enquire. Its foundation was an idea called **hypertext**, which made it possible for him to link documents that had words in common. It worked well for him, and Berners-Lee tried to convince others at CERN to try out his new program. Unfortunately, not many people took him up on his offer. His contract at CERN was only six months long, and soon Berners-Lee was off to a new job.

Berners-Lee's work at CERN didn't start out remarkable, but it led to bigger things!

Challenges at CERN

In 1981, Berners-Lee went to work for Image Computer Systems. He worked with graphics and communications software, and developed another computer language.

By 1984, Berners-Lee was back at CERN, but this time he had a much bigger challenge. People at the lab needed to be able to share their research documents with one another, but they didn't have group messaging systems like we use today. Each person had to communicate with another person one-on-one. Different programs had to be learned on different computers and software. Because the people who worked at CERN came from all over the world, so did their computers. Getting messages and information to an entire group was a huge task. "Often it was just easier to go and ask people when they were having coffee," said Berners-Lee.

At CERN, Berners-Lee had to figure out how to get many kinds of computers and software to communicate with one another.

A Big Idea

Berners-Lee made a good start at helping everyone communicate, but it wasn't enough. The Internet had been developed by this time, but it was very hard to find your way around it. This gave Berners-Lee an idea.

He wondered if he could write programs that could translate information from one system so that it could be put into another system, maybe even over and over again. Then he wondered if there was a better way to do it. The more he thought about it, he believed he could fix the problem for good. He thought, "Can't we **convert** every information system so that it looks like part of some imaginary information system which everyone can read?" That practical idea was what eventually became the World Wide Web.

Tim Berners-Lee is always thinking of ways to improve on the work he's already done.

Hype over HTTP

By 1989, Berners-Lee's idea was becoming a reality. It allowed people all over the world to share their research and ideas almost instantly. However, he didn't stop there. He worked with others at CERN to write something called **hypertext transfer protocol**, or HTTP. This was used for connecting documents over the Internet. HTTP controls all the communications between web servers—which is where documents are stored—and the browsers, or client programs, we use to look at them.

Finally, Berners-Lee invented an **application** that allowed users to view and change their documents online. Welcome to the World Wide Web! Anyone who worked at CERN had access to these new marvels by October 1990. It's hard to believe his creation didn't really turn many heads at first.

To organize work at CERN, Berners-Lee worked hard to create what would become the web, but it hardly got any notice at first.

Hello, WWW!

On August 6, 1991, Berners-Lee made his creation available to the public. He made his own website (info.cern.ch) accessible to everyone. He also included instructions for how to set up a website and servers. He even offered all the software he used. And all of this was free to anyone who wanted to use it!

To get the word out, Berners-Lee announced all this using a few mail groups on the Internet. Soon, computer fans all over the world found out about Berners-Lee's invention, and they were excited! They used his instructions to create websites. Then, they shared their work with Berners-Lee. In turn, he posted links to these new websites on his site for even more people to see.

Berners-Lee wasn't interested in making a lot of money. He just wanted everyone—from CERN employees to businesses to individuals—to be able to benefit from his invention.

The Web Is for Everyone!

Word about the World Wide Web spread like wildfire! People could share photos, documents, audio, and video on the web. They could download software. People started to create all kinds of websites. It wasn't just used by computer specialists anymore.

Because the web was clearly a big deal, others saw how it could be used to make money. However, from the beginning, Berners-Lee didn't want to use his invention for profit. He wanted the web to be free and open to anyone who wanted to use it. In 1994, he joined the Laboratory for Computer Science at the Massachusetts Institute of Technology (MIT). There, he created the World Wide Web Consortium (W3C). It's a group that oversees the web.

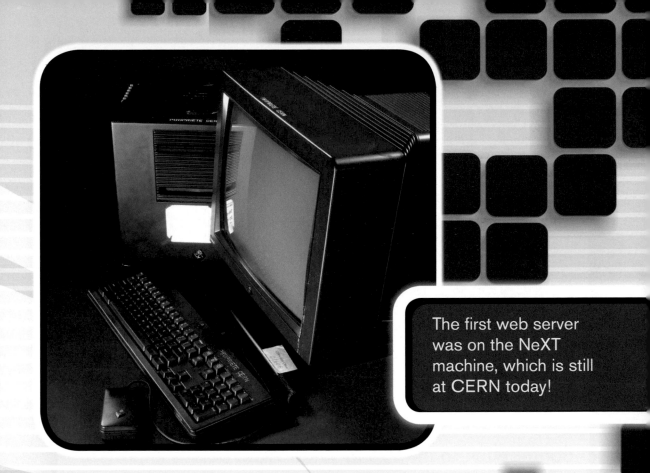

The first web server was on the NeXT machine, which is still at CERN today!

His Vision

When Berners-Lee invented the World Wide Web, he had grand visions for it. He wanted it to be used as a creative tool. Users would go on the web to create their own sites, using it as a tool. However, some of the most accessible browsers didn't allow people the ability to edit at first. This was a frustrating obstacle for Berners-Lee for many years. Now, websites such as Facebook allow people to post their own thoughts and creations in an easier way.

Sir Tim

Berners-Lee still has a vision for the web. In 2009, Berners-Lee founded the World Wide Web Foundation and became its director. The World Wide Web Foundation wants the web to be used to communicate, cooperate, and create freely. This group works to keep the web open to everyone and to make sure it helps humanity.

Tim Berners-Lee is pretty modest about his contribution to the World Wide Web, but it's important to us! We have come to use it and depend on it every day. In 2004, Queen Elizabeth II of the United Kingdom honored him with knighthood. He has won many other honors for his work, too. Without Sir Tim, the way we use the Internet would be very different!

Berners-Lee lives with his wife, Rosemary Leith. She plays a key role in the World Wide Web Foundation.

Sir Tim Is an Ordinary Guy

Even though he's known all around the world as the man who invented the World Wide Web—and a knight—Berners-Lee says he's just a normal guy. "I'm just an ordinary person with ordinary faults, who's difficult to talk to on Monday mornings when they're grumpy and things." Even the inventor of the web forgets things such as other people's names. And when he talks about his work, he emphasizes this: "It's been the spirit of collaboration."

Timeline

June 8, 1955
Tim Berners-Lee is born in London, England.

1976
Berners-Lee graduates from The Queen's College at Oxford University, England.

1980
Berners-Lee works for six months at CERN, where he invents the Enquire program.

1984
Berners-Lee returns to work at CERN.

1989
Berners-Lee invents the World Wide Web.

October 1990
The web is made available to everyone at CERN, but it doesn't get much attention.

November 12, 1990
Berners-Lee presents the idea of hyperlinks.

August 6, 1991
Berners-Lee makes his creation available to the public.

1994
Berners-Lee founds the World Wide Web Consortium (W3C).

1999
Berners-Lee is named one of *Time* magazine's "100 Most Important People of the 20th Century."

2004
Berners-Lee is knighted by Queen Elizabeth II.

2009
Berners-Lee founds the World Wide Web Foundation.

2013
Queen Elizabeth Prize for Engineering is awarded to Berners-Lee.

Glossary

access: To be able to use or enter something.

application: A program that performs one of the tasks for which a computer is used.

circuit: An electric current's full path.

commercial: Having to do with the buying and selling of goods and services.

convert: To change something into a different form so it can be used in a different way.

hypertext: A way to connect information to what is shown on a screen quickly, such as by a mouse click.

hypertext transfer protocol (HTTP): The information communication procedure used on the World Wide Web.

mainframe: A large, fast computer that has the ability to do many jobs at the same time.

particle physics: A division of physics that deals with the relations between pieces of matter that are smaller than atoms.

physics: The study of matter, energy, force, and motion, and the relationship among them.

software: Programs that run on computers and perform certain functions.

solder: To join two metallic surfaces by using a mix of melted metals.

telecommunications: Communication over a distance, such as by cable, telegraph, telephone, or broadcasting.

transistor: A device that can control the flow of electricity in electronics.

Index

Websites

Due to the changing nature of Internet links, PowerKids Press has developed an online list of websites related to the subject of this book. This site is updated regularly. Please use this link to access the list: www.powerkidslinks.com/compio/tbl